My Country, 'Tis of Thee

Ben Nussbaum

"My country..."

Some songs can make
people feel happy.
Some songs can make
people feel sad.
Some songs make people
feel proud of their country.

Jump into
Fiction

Bert's Big Day

Bert is nervous as he stands on the stage.
He sees his parents smiling from their chairs.

Mr. Jackson puts his hands up
to start.
Bert takes a deep breath.

"My country, 'tis of thee," Bert sings with the rest of his class. As the song goes on, he gets less and less nervous.

Instead, Bert is proud to sing! He is proud to sing for his country!

Back to Nonfiction

"'tis of thee..."

'Tis is an old way to say *it is*.

Thee means *you*.

This line means "it is about you, my country."

Who Wrote "America"?

Samuel Francis Smith wrote the words to this song.
He wrote it while he was a student.

"Sweet land of liberty, Of thee I sing."

The song calls America "sweet land of liberty."

Liberty means *freedom.*

It is good to be free!

This line of the song means, "I sing about my country, where I am free."

Many Countries, Other Words

The music for "America" is used in many countries.

Only the words change.

Those songs are special to those places.

"Land where my fathers died. Land of the pilgrims' pride."

The pilgrims were people who came to America a long time ago.

They wanted a new home.

They were not free in their old home.

They were proud of their new land.

They did not think about the land already belonging to other people.

A Day for Pilgrims

Pilgrims once ate a meal with an American Indian tribe. We still remember that meal. We call it Thanksgiving.

"From every mountain side..."

America is a big place.

A lot of people have lived there.

They have tried to make life better.

This song is for people all over the country.

Think and Talk

How does this song
make you feel?

"Let freedom ring!"

Americans are free.

They can agree with their leaders.

They can disagree with them too!

That is part of being free.

National Anthem

"America" is a special song.
But it is not the national anthem.
"The Star-Spangled Banner" is
the U.S. national anthem.

"America" says to let freedom ring
from every mountain side.
You can be proud about freedom.
Do not whisper you are free.
Shout it loud!
Let it ring!

America

America is a country where people are free.
It is where people can make their own choices.

People can start a business.
They can choose which holidays to celebrate.
They can move to a new home.
They are free to live their lives.

America can make people feel proud.
When people are proud of their country,
they want to make it the best it can be.
That is a good feeling!
So, sing loud and let it ring!

Civics in Action

Americans have symbols. These remind people of the country. The symbols make them proud. They make people think of freedom. The flag is a symbol for America.

1. You can hold a flag-raising service. You will raise a flag up a flagpole at the service. Decide what else you will do.

2. Invite others to come to the service.

3. Hold the service.